Winner of the Obie Award, the Lucille Lortel Award, five Craig Noel
Awards (San Diego), the Joseph Jefferson Award (Chicago),
the Gregory Award (Seattle), the Elliot Norton Award (Boston) and
Drama Desk nominations for Music and Solo Performance

"Smartly conceived and impressively executed, *An Iliad* relates an age-
old story that resonates with tragic meaning today."
—MICHAEL SOMMERS, *The New York Times*

"Absolutely riveting."   —ROBERT HURWITT, *San Francisco Chronicle*

"Drawing on the muscular translation by Robert Fagles, Mr. O'Hare and
Ms. Peterson have telescoped the mighty expanses of Homer's great
poem into an evening that scales the conflict of the Trojan War down to
an intimate solo show illuminating both the heroism and the horror of
warfare."   —CHARLES ISHERWOOD, *The New York Times*

"*An Iliad* is pure theater: shocking, glorious, primal and deeply
satisfying."   —DAVID COTE, *Time Out New York*

"In a mesmerizing play . . . Lisa Peterson and Denis O'Hare have
condensed the 24-book poem into 100 intelligent, emotional minutes
. . . a wrenching theatrical experience."
—JENNIFER FARRAR, *Associated Press*

"Listening to *An Iliad* in a manner that could be breathtakingly close to
the way its first audiences heard and saw it is a treat too good to miss."
—DAVID FINKLE, *The Huffington Post*

"The show is a sweeping, visceral theatrical event . . . commands
attention from start to finish."   —ANDY PROPST, *TheaterMania*

"A transformative act of theatrical magic."   —BOB VERINI, *Variety*

"A starkly powerful experience . . . The vernacular language mixed in with the soaring poetry of *An Iliad* collapses any sense of comfortable distance we may feel." —Don Aucoin, *The Boston Globe*

"*An Iliad* is unquestionably a victory of the theatrical imagination . . . The rhetoric soars for moments with battlefield exploits but then is brought back down to our contemporary idiom to close the gap between this ancient mythological world and our own." —Charles McNulty, *Los Angeles Times*

"This is poetry as it was meant to be experienced, primal and raw, thrilling and transcendent." —Jenny Lower, *LA Weekly*

"The act of combat has never been more piercingly described (not even by Tolstoy or Mailer . . .), nor its qualities of rage, savagery, and comradeship more intensely conveyed." —Myron Meisel, *The Hollywood Reporter*

"This is a formidably powerful piece of solo theater that evokes the rubble of history and of lessons mankind consistently fails to learn." —Chris Jones, *Chicago Tribune*

"Explosive, altogether breathtaking . . . Brilliantly meshes past and present calamity, with touches of the most caustic dark humor suddenly shifting into unimaginable pathos." —Hedy Weiss, *Chicago Sun-Times*

"Humor is an invaluable tool in this riveting one-actor adaptation of Homer's epic poem, easing the audience into the Poet's tale before he takes them on a devastating tour of the Trojan battlefield." —Oliver Sava, *Time Out Chicago*

"*An Iliad* demands a thinking audience." —Catey Sullivan, *Chicago Theater Beat*

"*An Iliad* tells the whole story in an artfully edited form that not only hits all the important plot points and set pieces but renders them with a deep consciousness of their ironies, agonies, subtleties, and implications." —TONY ADLER, *Chicago Reader*

"A triumph of theater." —LAWRENCE BOMMER, *Chicago Stage Style*

"O'Hare and Peterson mingle written and spoken ancient language with modern day grocery line descriptions. The that-was-then and this-is-still-how-it-is revelation is gut-punching." —KATY WALSH, *Chicago Now*

"Peterson and O'Hare illuminate, far better than any mere film, the guts and passion—the almost hallucinatory high of battle and that camaraderie between soldiers that noncombatants cannot comprehend." —GRAYDON ROYCE, *Minneapolis Star Tribune*

"*An Iliad* strips the varnish and the romance from war, offering a crystalline account of the horrors, the follies and the costs of armed conflict." —DOMINIC P. PAPATOLA, *St. Paul Pioneer Press*

"How incredibly powerful this work of theatre is . . ." —VAN BADHAM, *The Guardian*

"A breathtaking tour-de-force that begs the question: Has anything really changed since the Trojan War?" —STEPHEN HOUSE, *AussieTheatre.com*

"In the inspired hands of Denis O'Hare and Lisa Peterson, who have adapted Homer's masterpiece to encompass the war-glutted centuries that followed the Trojan campaign, we have a chance to hear the story told in such a way it feels as though we have never heard it before." —ELSPETH SANDYS, *New Zealand Listener*

Photo © Fred Hayes

Photo: Courtesy of the author

LISA PETERSON is an Obie-award winning director whose other compositions include a musical adaptation of Virginia Woolf's *The Waves*, with music by David Bucknam (New York Theater Workshop). In addition to many classic plays, Lisa has directed the premieres of new works by Donald Margulies, Tony Kushner, Beth Henley, Naomi Wallace, Jose Rivera, and others at theaters including NYTW (OBIE for directing Caryl Churchill's *Light Shining in Buckinghamshire*), Public, Vineyard, MTC, Primary Stages, Guthrie, ATL, Berkeley Rep, McCarter, Arena Stage, Geffen, Hartford Stage, Seattle Rep, and many more. Lisa was Associate Director at La Jolla Playhouse for three years and Resident Director at the Mark Taper Forum for ten years.

DENIS O'HARE is a Tony-award winning stage performer who has also appeared in television and film, including *Law & Order, True Blood*, and *American Horror Story,* for which he was nominated for an Emmy, *Michael Clayton, Dallas Buyers Club,* and *The Normal Heart*. His stage work includes *Take Me Out* (Tony Award, Best Performance by a Featured Actor), title role in *Uncle Vanya* Off-Broadway, *Elling*, and the musicals *Assassins, Cabaret, Sweet Charity* (Drama Desk Award), and the Shakespeare in the Park production of *Into the Woods*, with Amy Adams. Denis and Lisa are currently writing a new piece entitled *The Good Book*, an exploration of the evolution of the Bible. An avid artist, fierce progressive, and activist, his happiest role is as a father to his son.

ROBERT FAGLES (1933-2008) was Professor of Comparative Literature Emeritus at Princeton University. He was the recipient of the 1997 PEN/ Ralph Manheim Medal for Translation. His acclaimed translations include Aeschylus' *Oresteia* (nominated for a National Book Award), Virgil's *Aeneid*, and Homer's *Iliad*.

AN ILIAD

Lisa Peterson
and Denis O'Hare

Based on Homer's *Iliad*,
Translated by Robert Fagles

Overlook Duckworth
New York • London

This edition first published in the United States and the United Kingdom
in 2014 by Overlook Duckworth, Peter Mayer Publishers, Inc.

New York
141 Wooster Street
New York, NY 10012
www.overlookpress.com
For bulk and special sales, please contact sales@overlookny.com,
or write us at above address.

London
30 Calvin Street
London E1 6NW
info@duckworth-publishers.co.uk
www.ducknet.co.uk
For bulk and special sales, please contact sales@duckworth-publishers.co.uk,
or write us at the above address.

Cataloging-in-Publication Data is available from the Library of Congress
A catalogue record for this book is available from the British Library

Book design and type formatting by Bernard Schleifer
Manufactured in the United States of America
ISBN 978-1-4683-0808-2 (US)
ISBN 978-0-7156-4740-0 (UK)
3 5 7 9 10 8 6 4

Do not envy the violent
or choose any of their ways.

—Book of Proverbs 3:31

Lisa Peterson and Denis O'Hare working at Sundance Institute, July 2009.

AUTHORS' NOTE

A work as monumental as Homer's *Iliad* is not easily reducible to one or two themes. To say that it is about the glory of war is as wrong-headed as saying that it is an anti-war tract. When we started grappling with this work, attempting to form our own theatrical narrative, we did so using two distinct lenses: the lens of pacifism—summed up by the idea that war is a waste, and should be eradicated; and the lens of humanism—the idea that human nature is warlike, and can't be changed. We let these two tensions battle it out in the person of our narrator and we threaded our way through the many chapters of Homer's great work with these impulses in mind.

As we developed *An Iliad*, we began to understand that what we were after was, in fact, very old-fashioned. Since our desire was to give an audience the sensation of being present at the very invention of this epic story, we found ourselves hearkening back to the bards of old, recalling campfire mesmerists, ghost-story purveyors, even con-men. Our narrator is one of a long line of vagabonds, or perhaps he is the original vagabond: a man (or woman) who ekes out a living by begging a crowd to stop, listen, and imagine for a while.

We began talking about performing *The Iliad* not long after the United States invaded Iraq in 2003. We were both thinking about war, and plays about war—thinking that at the time, the best thing a theater artist could do was to find a way to talk about what it means to be a country at war. Most people think of *The Iliad* as an epic poem, not a play. We had both studied it as a work of literature, not a piece of theater—but the more we read about the ancient oral tradition and

Homer, the more convinced we became that the staggering tale of the Trojan War really was spoken out loud and passed from storyteller to storyteller for centuries before it was ever written down. We began to imagine a character called The Poet: an ancient teller of tales who might still exist in the universe, doomed to tell the story of the Trojan War until the day when human nature changes, when our addiction to rage comes to an end, when the telling of a war story becomes unnecessary. A day that has yet to come, of course.

We imagine that our Poet traveled across the wine-dark seas with Agamemnon and Achilles and the Greek armies. That he camped there on the coast of Ilium for nine years with the Greek soldiers, that he did lay eyes on Troy and fell in love with that culture. That he has roamed the world telling the story of Achilles and Hector and Hecuba and Hermes and all the hundreds of other characters that inhabit *The Iliad*. He has told this story for thousands of years, and in that time he has witnessed (or thinks, or imagines, he has witnessed) every war from the Trojan War onwards. He's found himself at each battle, in every trench, at every wall, in the mess halls, in the infirmaries, over the centuries. He has wandered the scorched battlefields and befriended—then lost— soldiers in all corners of the world's history, witnessing and recording everything. He's a compendium of war.

We imagine that on this particular night, our Poet finds himself transported to an empty stage, in front of a particular audience, and he chooses to tell the story in this way: as an inexorable collision between two great warriors—Achilles and Hector—and that on this particular night he becomes infected with rage himself, and nearly loses himself in a telescopic listing of all wars ever fought, and that on this night he tries to quit telling the story, but can't. We think that he still believes in the old gods, and that the old gods won't let him quit. They won't let him out of his storytelling purgatory.

Homer's *Iliad* begins with the Poet asking the muses to help him, and throughout the epic poem you can find these invocations. We decided to make the Muse actually appear, and to us that means that music literally enters the world near the top of our Part Two. The inclusion of music in this piece is not just incidental. It is a vital part of the evening's progress; we view the muse as the other major character in the play. In the McCarter and New York Theatre Workshop productions we used an extraordinary string bass player named Brian Ellingsen to embody this Muse. The back-and-forth dialogue between The Poet and the Musician was a real duet, and we would encourage other directors to either license Mark's Bennett's gorgeous score, or to explore using music in some other way.

We imagine there are many ways to approach this script. We've had the great pleasure of seeing quite a few remarkable actors tackle this piece, and succeed. We look forward to that community of Poets expanding in every direction; there is no reason that The Poet could not be female, or any race, or differently-abled, or over 70 or under 30. We think of Homer as a kind of coat that anyone with the passion and the talent (and the ability to memorize) the story could wear. Though we definitely invented this play to be performed by a lone figure, we recognize that it could be performed by more than one person, and would encourage people to find their own way.

We've been working on *An Iliad* for nearly ten years, and over that time the nexus of world conflict has shifted, of course. When we started, the U.S. had just invaded Iraq. Today, that war is officially over, but Afghanistan still rumbles, and around the globe new conflicts have made themselves known. For that reason, we recognize that are a few places in the script where, over time, there might need to be a bit of adjustment in order to stay current. We've noted those places in the script, with guidelines for keeping up to date.

And finally, we fell in love with Robert Fagles's glorious translation. To us, it remains the most compelling and playable English version of the poetry of *The Iliad*. It is written in fairly free dactylic hexameter—very different from the iambic pentameter that we're all used to in the English language theater. In this script, we have indented the Fagles verse to set it off from the rest of the text. We highly recommend the introductions that Fagles and his editor Bernard Knox have included in their full editions of *The Iliad*, and would certainly recommend that anyone taking on this project read the entire Fagles translation of the epic.

An Iliad started out as an examination of war and man's tendency toward war. In the end, it also became an examination of the theater and the way in which we still tell each other stories in order to try to make sense of ourselves, and our behavior. Someone started telling the story of the Trojan War, in all its glory and devastation and surprise, over 3,000 years ago. We pass it on.

ACKNOWLEDGMENTS

We were counseled very wisely by a number of people over the years, as we worked on *An Iliad*. We would never have had the idea without the wisdom of our friend Morgan Jeness. And we wouldn't have perfected the Poet's voice without the eagle eye of our dramaturg, Janice Paran. Many thanks to them, and to Philip Himberg, Christopher Hibma and the Sundance family; Jerry Manning and the Seattle Repertory Theater; Emily Mann, Mara Issacs and the McCarter Theater; Jim Nicola, Linda Chapman, and the team at NYTW; Lynne Fagles, Professor James Tatum, Professor Olga Levaniouk, Hans Altwies, and Stephen Spinella.

PERFORMANCES

An Iliad was developed in part with the assistance of the Sundance Institute Theatre Program.

An Iliad was originally produced by Seattle Repertory Theatre (Jerry Manning, Producing Artistic Director; Benjamin Moore, Managing Director) in Seattle, Washington, opening on April 9, 2010. It was directed by Lisa Peterson; the set design was by Rachel Hauck; the costume design was by Marcia Dicxy Jory; the lighting design was by Scott Zielinski; the original music and sound design were by Paul James Prendergast; the stage manager was Michael B. Paul; and the dramaturg was Janice Paran. The production featured Hans Altwies as The Poet.

An Iliad was produced at the McCarter Theatre Center (Emily Mann, Artistic Director; Timothy J. Shields, Managing Director; Mara Isaacs, Producing Director) in Princeton, New Jersey, opening on October 29, 2010. It was directed by Lisa Peterson; the set design was by Rachel Hauck; the costume design was by Marina Draghici; the lighting design was by Scott Zielinski; and the original music and sound design were by Mark Bennett and the production stage manager was Cheryl Mintz. The production featured Brian Ellingsen as The Musician and Stephen Spinella as The Poet.

An Iliad was produced at New York Theater Workshop (James C. Nicola, Artistic Director; William Russo, Managing Director) in New York City, opening on March 7, 2012. It was directed by Lisa Peterson; the set design was by Rachel Hauck; the costume design was by Marina Draghici; the lighting design was by Scott Zielinski; the original music and sound design were by Mark Bennett; and the production stage manager was Donald Fried. The production featured Brian Ellingsen as The Musician and Denis O'Hare and Stephen Spinella as The Poet on alternate nights.

Opening night at New York Theatre Workshop, February 2012. From left to right: Stephen Spinella, Marina Draghici, Denis O'Hare, Lisa Peterson, Mark Bennett, Brian Ellingsen, Rachel Hauck.

Hans Altwies, Seattle Repertory Theatre, 2010.

Denis in reading at Sundance Institute, July 2010.

AN ILIAD

CHARACTERS

THE POET

PART ONE
THE ARMIES GATHER

Denis O'Hare.

An empty space. Dim light. Suddenly, a door in the back wall opens and a MAN *enters. He's wearing an old coat, a hat pulled down over his eyes, and carrying a suitcase. There is something ancient about him, but it may just be that he looks weary, as if he's been traveling for a very long time. He walks toward us, puts down the suitcase. He squints out at us, taking us in. Hesitates, not entirely sure if he's in the right place.*

The MAN *shakes his head, closes his eyes, gathers his energy, and begins:*

POET

μῆνιν ἄειδε θεὰ Πηληϊάδεω Ἀχιλῆος'
MEH nin ah | EI de the | A PEH | LEH ia | DYO akhi | LEH os
οὐλομένην, ἣ μυρί' Ἀχαιοῖς ἄλγε' ἔθηκε
OU lo me | NEHN HEH | MU ri a | KHAI OIS | AL ge' eh | THEH ke
πολλὰς δ'ἰφθίμους ψυχὰς Ἄϊδι προΐαψεν
PO LLAS | D'IPH THI | MOUS PSU | KHAS ah i | DI pro i | AH psen
ἡρώων,
HEH RO | ON —

[*Translation:*
Rage—Goddess, sing the rage of Peleus' son Achilles,
murderous, doomed, that cost the Acheans countless losses,
hurling down to the House of Death so many sturdy souls,
great fighters' souls—]

23

(He stops, lost. He looks out at us, embarrassed. He shuffles down to the edge of the stage, and peers out into the dark. He squints and examines the audience.)

Back then, oh I could sing it. For days and nights. On and on, every battle, every old digression, I would sing and sing . . . in Mycenae once I sang for a year—you don't believe me? In Babylon, I sang it differently, but the crowds came . . . in Alexandria I started to notice a few empty seats, but still I sang it. Shorter though—three or four days. Know where it went down really well? Gaul, something about those people, they had a real taste for it—of course they were hard to control, they used to get up on tables and sing along, they threatened to take the whole thing over, went outside, screaming, building fires, terrible.

Every time I sing this song, I hope it's the last time.

(With Homeric intensity.) Ohhh, sing to me now. Uhhh, you muses. In the halls of Olympus . . . you are goddesses! You are everywhere! You know everything! All we hear is the distant ring of glory . . . *(Hopefully.)* Sing!

(Suddenly changing subject—a diversion.) You know, in the old days, we'd be in a tavern, or a bar, I guess you would say. It was so much easier to talk about these horrors in a bar . . . *(He takes off his hat and looks toward the suitcase.)* This is the story of the Trojan War. And two great fighters—Achilles and Hector—

(Imploring.) Ohhhhh . . . Muses . . .

RAGE

(He concentrates very hard, searching his memory and asking the Muses to help. He closes his eyes.)

μῆνιν ἄειδε θεὰ Πηληϊάδεω Ἀχιλῆος'
MEH nin ah | EI de the | A PEH | LEH ia | DYO akhi | LEH os
οὐλομένην,
OU lo me | NEHN …

(Waits. Then, in a burst of inspiration, he squeezes out six lines of dactylic hexameter.)

RAGE!

Goddess, sing the rage of Peleus' son Achilles,
Murderous, doomed, that cost the Achaeans countless losses,
Hurling down to the House of Death so many sturdy souls,
Great fighters' souls, but made their bodies carrion,
Feasts for the dogs and birds . . .

What drove them to fight with such a fury?

Ohhh . . . the gods, of course . . . um . . . pride, honor, jealousy . . . Aphrodite . . . some game or other, an apple, Helen being more beautiful than somebody—it doesn't matter. The point is, Helen's been stolen, and the Greeks have to get her back.

(Tired by the idea of it.) Huhhh. It's always something, isn't it . . . ?

But—it's a good story. I—I remember a lot of it, I remember a lot of it.

Imagine a beach—rocky, jagged—and oh about a mile and a half inland imagine a city, with stone ramparts protecting it. This city was

Memory

called Troy, and from the walls of this city Hector can see the water, down by the beach, and in that water, there are hundreds of ships. It is crowded with all kinds of Greek ships. This is where my story takes place. Ages ago.

(*With Homeric intensity.*) Who were the captains of those Greek ships? Who were the captains of Achaea? Ahhhhh! The mass of troops I could never tally, I could, I could, if . . . if I had ten tongues in ten mouths . . . if, if, if, if I, if I had a heart made of me bronze. (*He likes that.*) Yes! A heart made of me bronze. And if I could remember the names, that is—if I could actually remember everybody.

> Sing! Sing in memory
> All who gathered under Troy . . .

The List of Ships . . . the numbers of men on those ships . . . Muses?

(*No answer from the Muses. He concentrates very hard—willing his memory to wake up—and slowly at first, he calls up the list of ships.*)

Here goes:

> First came the Boeotian units led by Lay-i-tus and Pen-e-lay-os:
> Ar-se-si-lay-us and Proth-o-ee-nor and Clonius shared command
> Of the armed men who lived in Hyria, rocky Aulis . . .
> (*Grasping, he skips ahead.*) Thespia and Gray-uh, the dancing
>   rings of My-ka-less-us,
> Men who lived round Harma, Il-e-si-on and Er-y-three . . .
> (*Skips ahead again.*) Co-pae, Eu-tree-sis and Thisbe thronged
>   with doves—

Ah, it's coming back to me, yes (*He picks up the pace . . .*)

sad

Fighters from Coronea, Haleartus deep in meadows,
And the men who held Plataea and lived in Glisas,
Men who held the rough-hewn gates of Lower Thebes,
On-kee-stus the holy, Poseidon's sun-filled grove,
Men from the town of Arne green with vineyards . . .

(*He stops himself.*) Ah, that's right, you don't know any of these places
. . . but these names—these names mean something to me. And I
knew these boys . . .

The point is, on all these ships, are boys from every small town in Ohio,
from farmlands, from fishing villages . . . the boys of Nebraska and
South Dakota . . . the twangy boys of Memphis . . . the boys of San
Diego, Palo Alto, Berkeley, Antelope Valley . . . You can imagine, you
can imagine, you know, um . . . there are soldiers from Kansas. There
are soldiers from Lawrence, Kansas.* There are soldiers from Spring-
field, Illinois. Evanston, Illinois. Chicago, Illinois. Buffalo, New York. Coo-
perstown, New York. Brooklyn, Queens, Staten Island, uh, the Bronx,
South Bronx. You have soldiers from Florida, from the Panhandle, with
its snake charmers and evangelists, from the Okeechobee. You have
soldiers from Miami who speak Spanish, Miami who speak French, Miami who speak English. You have Puerto Rican soldiers. You have soldiers from Texas, from the flatland, from Dallas, from Plano, from Hous-
ton. There are soldiers from Tennessee, from western Tennessee, from
the mountains, from the mountains in Virginia, the mountains in Seattle.
From Flint, Michigan, from Benton Harbor, from—from—from—in the
thumb, from Escanaba, you know what I mean? . . . That's it. That's it.

* We like to include one or two towns from the locale where the play is being performed. Feel free to pick a couple of nearby places that produce enlisted men and
women, and insert them after Lawrence, Kansas.

memory

You get the point.

 Known and unknown.

We're talking tens of thousands of men, emptied out of the Greek islands.

Picture these men, these ships, so many ships.

(*He begins to count the ships as he sees them in his mind's-eye, drawing attention to his favorite commanders.*) 50, 40, 40, 40, 50, 80, 100—Agamemnon—60, 40, 40, 12—Odysseus—80, 30, 50—Achilles—11, 40, 30—these are ships I'm counting, not men—40, 40, 90—Nestor . . . that's, how many, uhhhhh, hundreds and hundreds of ships . . .

That's 120 men on each ship . . . tens of thousands, hundreds of thousands of Greek men. Do you see?

(*Silence.*)

So here we are—

Nine years.

(*Beat.*) Oh please . . . O Muses . . . don't make me do this alone. (*No answer.*) Nine years.

 Fighting on and off, fighting to the wall and back. Greeks win one day, Trojans win the next, like a game of tug-of-war, and nothing to show for it but exhaustion, poverty, and loneliness.

What was it like? Ah, it was a pain. It was awful. It was, it was, it was hot. How about that? It was hot. How can I—?

Nine years. So for—so you left home when your baby was one, you come back and your baby is ten. You left your baby was one, you come back your baby is dead. You come back your—your wife is dead. You come back your wife is fat. You come back your wife has had three affairs and two more kids. "Uh, hi honey, y-uhhhhh, don't get mad, don't get mad." You know, or you come back, and the farm is ruined. Or there's been a war and you're no longer Greek. You're now Diocletian or whatever it is—you're Spartan now. They came and took over, while you were hanging out at Troy, and you have no title to your land anymore. Um, your father died while you were gone. You know, oh no (*gasp*) we don't wear those leggings anymore, we stopped wearing them like that a long time ago . . .

And so, you can imagine, after nine years of this, well, they want to go home. They've forgotten why they're fighting.

> —But what humiliation it would be
> To hold out so long, then sail home empty handed.

How do you know when you've won? You know, someone said, uh how do you ask uh a person to be the last man to die for a, for a—a losing cause and I, I'm paraphrasing but the idea being, you're in the super-market line, and you've been there for twenty minutes and the other line's moving faster. Do you switch lines now? No, goddamn it, I've been here for twenty minutes, I'm gonna wait in this line, I don't care if I wait. And look—I'm not leaving 'cuz otherwise I've wasted my time.

> Courage, my friends, hold out a little longer . . .

The poet explains all his memories of the war.

Stephen Spinella and Denis O'Hare in front of
New York Theatre Workshop, March 2012.

PART TWO

ACHILLES

Stephen Spinella, NYTW, 2012.

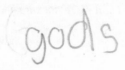

POET Now this whole time, of course, the gods were watching. Up on Mount Olympus. And some of them cheered on the Greeks—"Achilles!" And some of them cheered on the Trojans—"Hector!" Like sports fans. And really, back then, this was their only entertainment, they were addicted to it, they couldn't allow it to end, and so they'd swoop down and pinch and prod and whisper, just to make sure the battles kept raging. Ah, the old gods. You remember Zeus? And his wife, Hera? Apollo? Athena? (*Looking out at us.*) No? Well, they haven't been around.

(*He opens the suitcase, takes out a bottle, pours.*)

Where do the old gods go? That's a song. (*Sings.*) "Where do the old gods go when they die?" I don't know. There's one in the gin bottle, there's one in the vodka bottle . . . Spirits. Oh look, Athena in the . . . she's in the tequila. (*Giggling.*) Yeah. Athena tequila. (*Contemplating the bottle—enjoying the mystery.*) Gods never die. They change. They, they, they *burrow* inside us . . . They *become* us, they become our *impulses.* (*He seems to call on the audience.*) Lust? Aphrodite. Mischief? Hermes. A good idea? Athena . . .

Athena tequila. Ah very good. (*Another drink.*)

Oh, the things the gods could do to us.

(*Distant music, so faint that we're not sure if it's really there.*)

Muses?!

(*Suddenly a Muse appears and the world is full of sound and light. This could mean recorded music, or a live musician, but however it happens,* THE POET*'s world changes completely.*)

Nine years in. And we're all camped out on that beach. Bad enough. Only now it's night and men are suddenly getting VERY sick. One minute they're polishing their boots, the next they're choking on black blood. Down the beach, there's a massive fire burning, and the fire is not wood, it's corpses, they're burning the corpses of men and mules and dogs, they've all been infected by plague. *What is going on?*

I'll tell you: we've angered the gods. Agamemnon, our leader, our commander, has taken as the spoils of war this girl—gorgeous, fifteen years old—and she happens to be the daughter of a priest, a priest of *Apollo*.

The old man comes to Agamemnon with a cart piled high: "Please take these gifts, this ransom. Just give me back my daughter." Agamemnon says no. The priest offers to pray for the Greeks if only he'll give him his daughter back. Agamemnon says no. All of the Greek commanders come to Agamemnon and they beg him to give her back. Agamemnon says no.

The priest is heartsick, he goes to Apollo and Apollo gets mad.

Ever seen an angry god? (*Shakes his head.*) Apollo takes these arrows, and he covers the tips in sickness, in plague. Nasty stuff.

Anger

The arrows clanged at his back as the god quaked with rage,
Over against the ships he dropped to a knee, let fly a shaft
And a terrifying clash rang out from the great silver bow—

(THE POET *shoots a plague arrow, and another, and another.*) TUNG!!
TUNG!! TUNG!!

Infection. Disease. Death.

There's only one way to end the plague: Agamemnon has to give the
girl back.

AGAMEMNON
　　I won't give up the girl!

POET He's the commander, no one's going to tell *him* what to do. So
the Greeks call a *grand assembly*. Allll the tribes, allll the factions, allll
the warriors gather and

　　the meeting grounds shook,

everybody buzzing like, like bees, you know? They're angry and fright-
ened and sick of the plague—and Agamemnon sweeps in. All the men
shout, "Respect the priest! Take the ransom! Give her back!" Someone
yells "Quiet, quiet, quiet! The King of Men, Agamemnon is speaking!"

Silence.

Agamemnon grabs the scepter and rises:

AGAMEMNON OK—(*Magnanimously.*) —

I'm willing to give her back, if that's what you all want. I'm not a tyrant. I can see that it's best for everyone if I do.

> But fetch me another prize—and straight off too—
> else I alone of the Argives go without my honor.
> That would be a disgrace.

POET   And the men all kind of murmur 'cause there are no prizes left, they've all been distributed—someone will have to give up their prize—and suddenly a huge figure rises in the back—AH! (*Excited whisper.*) This is our man—

Achilles.

In the middle of all this—misery—there is this one genius.

Achilles . . . is the GREATEST WARRIOR that *ever* lived—bigger than Heracles, bigger than Sinbad, bigger than . . . (*Asking the audience.*) well, who's the greatest warrior living now . . . ? (*He waits for an answer and then quickly moves on.*) And he's not just good at killing. It's that he's good at the *art* of war. Now—you have to understand that Achilles is superhuman. He's, uh, half mortal, but also half god. His mother, Thetis, is a sea-nymph, he was raised by a centaur and, you know, amazing things, like his, his, he could talk to, he could understand animals. Animals talked to him. His horse—I can't remember the horse's name—talked to him. I remember wuh, once, once his horse sat him down. His horse said—no, no, one day, Achilles was, he was, he was uh, he was really . . . he was overeating, and his horse said, (*Neighing.*) "Whoa-oa-oa-oa!" (*Laughs.*) . . . We all laughed.

Oh yes . . . and Achilles knows he's going to die—here, in Troy. He doesn't know *when*, he doesn't know *how*, but he knows he won't be going home. That's been prophesied. Achilles will have a brief but *glorious* life. Imagine living with that.

This is Achilles. Here he is.

(THE POET *rises, transforms to embody Achilles.*)

ACHILLES

Just how, Agamemnon,
Great field marshal . . . most grasping man alive,
How can the generous Argives give you prizes now?
I know of no troves of treasure, piled, lying idle,
anywhere. Whatever we dragged from towns we plundered,
all's been portioned out. But collect it, call it back
from the rank and file? That would be the disgrace—

POET And oh—he shouldn't have said that, the men start to shrink back now, leaving Achilles alone to face the commander-in-chief.

AGAMEMNON You can't talk to me like that, even if you are the bravest fighter we have. You're so gifted. You're such a great warrior. But don't forget you're half god. I'm only a man, but I'll show you who's greater.

What do you want? To cling to your own prize
while I sit calmly by—empty-handed here?
I'll take what I want—Give me Briseis!

POET Now Briseis is someone that Achilles won, fair and square. Not only has he won her, he's come to love her. Briseis is his companion— she cooks for him, she sleeps with him, she's, she's become dear to him.

37

Rage

ACHILLES

Don't give me commands!

The Trojans never did me damage, not in the least.

No, you colossal, shameless—we all followed you,

to please you, to fight for you, to win your honor

back from the Trojans—Menelaus and you, you dog-face!

POET   The men all gasp!

ACHILLES

Never once did you arm with the troops and go to battle

  or risk an ambush—

You lack the courage, you can see death coming.

Safer by far, you find, to foray all through camp,

commandeering the prize of any man who speaks against you.

King who devours his people!

I have no mind to linger here, disgraced,

brimming your cup and piling up your plunder!

POET   He starts to leave—

AGAMEMNON

Desert, by all means—if the spirit drives you home!

I will never beg you to stay, not on my account.

But let this be my warning on your way:

I will be there in person at your tents

To take Briseis in all her beauty, your own prize—

So you can learn just how much greater I am than you

and the next man up may shrink from matching words with me!

POET   And Achilles flies into a RAGE:

38

Fur*ious*, Power

He grabs the scepter—now this scepter is, is, a Greek tradition, whenever anybody wants to speak officially we take the scepter—it's like a talking stick, the origins of democratic process and all of that—and Achilles says: "By this scepter, this mighty oak, that will never again flower, I swear, I will never fight again! Let all the Greeks die, let all the men be swept, not until, and, and let you, Agamemnon come on your knees to me, repentant, blubbering, wishing you had never said these words, you can eat your heart out, you can eat your words, I will never fight for you again. Trojan Hector will slaughter you all, you dare to humiliate, humiliate me?"—He raises his arm against Agamemnon. All the men are staring at him. What is he doing? And suddenly . . . his head yanks back. The men can't see what Achilles can see: Athena has grabbed him by the hair, she whispers in his ear, *"Hold back. You can't kill Agamemnon." . . .* And Achilles says, "Why?" And she says, *"Obey."*

Achilles has no choice. He takes the scepter and he BSHHHH to the ground, smashes it in pieces—not really, but—Furious! "None of you in this meeting will speak for me? See how you do without me."

And he storms out. And all the Greek army is standing there going, *(He shows us—slack-jawed.)* and Agamemnon's kinda going "Who the fuck cares about him?" And *he* leaves.

This is the rage of Peleus' son, Achilles.

(Nodding, confirming, calling it up.)

μῆνιν ἄειδε θεὰ Πηληϊάδεω Ἀχιλῆος'
MEH nin ah | EI de the | A PEH | LEH ia | DYO akhi | LEH os

MAD

(THE POET *pours another glass.*)

And there it is . . . that's how it starts, it's so . . . it's infuriating.

(*Drinks half the glass—he'd rather not tell us this, but he does.*)

They take the girl to Agamemnon's tent . . .

> And Achilles wept, and slipping away from his companions,
> far apart, sat down on the beach of the heaving gray sea
> and scanned the endless ocean.

(*Shakes his head.*) So . . . the war rages on, but Achilles stays in his tent. Waiting, fuming, betting against his own side, the Greeks.

(THE POET *drains his glass, then pours again—a big pour* . . . THE POET *looks up, smiles.*)

Agamemnon and
Achilles have a
huge fight.

PART THREE

HECTOR

Denis O'Hare, NYTW, 2012.

peace

POET   I wish I could show you a photograph of Troy. But here is what it was like:

Walk through the Scaean Gates and the first thing you'll see is a great plaza, a great plaza with a fountain, there's water everywhere: little waterfalls, little pools, every house has its own pool and you hear the sound of water flowing all the time and the water is a form of music, and that music mingles with real music: flutes, lyres, singing. And then as you walk through, you begin to see how every house is both private and public. So every house has a private area and yet it spills into a common area, so as you're walking through the city of Troy you see everybody, and everybody sees you. They'll often have events, they like to have their concerts, they have public meetings, they have performances of all kinds and there's a great sense of civic duty, so they get together to discuss things like: what do we do with the fig tree that's dying? How do we save the fig tree? And they have a committee to talk about the fig tree. And of course, respect for the family, the royal family, Priam and his sons. They've actually brought Troy peace, they've actually fought off invasions, they've actually given them a life that's stable. So what you feel when you walk into Troy is a great sense of calm and a great sense of serenity . . . this is before the war, of course.

Now the man called Hector.

43

(*Struggling.*) Shining Hector. Man-killing Hector. Hektoros hippo-damoio. (*He translates.*) Hector breaker of horses—it's always so hard to describe Hector—

His little brother calls him a "sharp ax"—a sharp edge, always cleaving forward . . .

Hector believes in—he believes in institutions, he believes in—in country, he believes in family, he believes in the army. Isn't it funny how hard it is to describe a good man?

He's a brave man, but deep down, he'd rather be taming horses.

But Hector is the eldest—first born and he's got DOZENS, and I mean DOZENS of brothers and sisters, more than fifty, by various mothers, I can't remember all their names now—my god—I would have to look that up, it's all written down somewhere . . . (*He digs through his suitcase, to no avail.*) But one brother especially—Paris—every time Hector sees Paris he can't seem to stop yelling at him. And for good reason, of course, because Paris was the kind of—(*Really enjoying himself.*) Paris actually figured out a way to make the case that it was better for him to stay inside, with the women, than go out and fight. And even when he did try to fight—once—Aphrodite swooped in and picked him up by the scruff of his neck, wrapped him in a blanket made of fog, and tossed him back in Helen's bed. And he stayed there. That's who Paris was. It, it was something like you know, "Ohhh, but if I go, and if they catch me, you know they will hold me for ransom and then you'll be put in an awkward position. Better for me to stay here and, and, you know, live out my days knowing that I am a coward and . . . " You know you couldn't argue with someone like that because he actually made the case for you and you were like . . . uhh . . . you are a coward, you know what I mean? But he had already called himself a coward—where are you going to go from there?

(*Leaning in.*) Everyone always wants to hear more about Paris, "Paris! Paris! Tell us more about Paris!" But actually, Paris isn't really that important—I know, I know, he stole Helen away from Menelaus and brought her to Troy and that started the war, and yes, he was SO HANDSOME and everything—but he's not interesting. Not interesting to me.

Anymore.

(*More serious now.*) But Hector.

You know, the thing about Hector is: He's *proud*. He won't let anyone else lead the charge for Troy. They've got allies, come in from all over, but Hector won't let them lead their own tribes. He wants to be in charge. Complicated. Full of hubris, but also decent.

Hector's a good husband, and a good father. He's a lot like . . . (*He trails off. The Muse urges him onward.*)

One terrible day—the Trojans are struggling—because the Greek army is full of ferocious warriors—Great Ajax, Diomedes—and even though Achilles won't fight, the Greeks are winning because Athena . . . oh, the gods have made a mess of things, you wouldn't believe all the . . . Athena even puts on her helmet and fights for the Greeks, stabbing her own brother Ares in the stomach, and he goes crying to Zeus—no, no, it's a mess . . .

On this day the Greeks, with the help of Athena, they hack and chop and decimate the Trojans, pushing them back toward the city walls.

Hector and his brothers try to hold their ground but they keep getting pushed back, pushed back, and Hector becomes afraid that the Trojan soldiers might give up and run away, or hide inside the city gates. Hector and one of his brothers—uh . . . (*Shrugs off trying to name him.*)—realize that they have to get Athena on their side. So Hector runs alone back toward Troy to ask the citizens to pray to Athena.

His mother, Hecuba, catches sight of him and runs and grabs his hand.

HECUBA

> My child—why have you left the bitter fighting,
> why have you come home? Look how they wear you out . . .
> But wait, I'll bring you some honeyed, mellow wine.
> When a man's exhausted, wine will build his strength—

HECTOR

> Don't offer me mellow wine, Mother, not now—
> you'd sap my limbs, I'd lose my nerve for war.

No—pray to the gods—ask Athena to stop helping the Greeks.

POET   And he runs on. Then "the face that launched a thousand ships," Helen—she stops him:

HELEN

> My dear brother,
> dear to me, bitch that I am, vicious, scheming—
> horror to freeze the heart! Oh how I wish
> that first day my mother brought me into the light
> some black whirlwind had rushed me out to the mountains!
> But since the gods ordained it all, these desperate years,
> I wish I had been the wife of a better man.

46

Family

But come in, rest on this seat with me, dear brother.
You are the one hit hardest by the fighting, Hector,
you more than all—and all for me, whore that I am,
and this blind mad Paris. Oh the two of us!

POET   But Hector doesn't have time for this, the only one he wants
to see is his wife, Andromache, and his son, Astyanax, who's just, oh,
maybe six months old . . . he goes to his house and they're not there, he
looks for them everywhere, he can't find them, he's starting to panic,
then someone tells him they're up on the tower, on the walls of the city,
and he runs up there, helmet flashing—still in his full armor. There they
are, his wife, Andromache, and his baby boy.

Hector smiles—that's a rare thing.

ANDROMACHE   Oh Hector. Why are you just staring at us? Can't
you speak?

(*Hector only shakes his head at their beauty. He doesn't know what
to say.*)

What are you doing home in the middle of the day? (*Smiling.*) Is the
war over?

HECTOR   (*A little laugh.*) No. It's a bad day for us. I've come home
to start the prayers.

ANDROMACHE   Oh.

Hector—please listen to me. You're all I have—Achilles killed my
mother, my father, my brothers. Now I have only you—and our child.

Family

I'm begging you—stay on the ramparts. Why can't you draw your army up by that fig tree down there, where the gate is weakest—you know they've attacked us three times on that very spot where the wall is low.

HECTOR   But that would make me look like a coward. I can't retreat—even though every night I wake in a sweat, dreaming of you widowed, enslaved, and the boy—

POET   Hector reaches for the baby—but Astyanax suddenly wails —WAHHHH!

HECTOR   What? What did I do?

ANDROMACHE   (*Laughing.*) It's your helmet! Take it off! Take it off!

HECTOR   (*Laughing, taking off his helmet.*) No, no, no, don't be afraid—that's only Daddy's helmet! Here—(*Lifting the child.*) Some day you'll wear a helmet like that. Some day you'll be an even greater soldier than your father. You'll ride a big horse, a dark one, just like mine. You'll fly on that horse, through the air! You'll come home wearing the bloody gear of the mortal enemy you've killed in battle—

ANDROMACHE (*Lightly, snatching Astyanax back.*) That's enough!

Reckless one,
Hector—your fiery courage will destroy you.
Have you no pity for him, our helpless son? Or me,
and the destiny that weighs me down, your widow,
now so soon—

HECTOR

Andromache why so desperate?
No man will hurl me down to Death, against my fate.
And fate? No one alive has ever escaped it,
neither brave man nor coward, I tell you—
it's born with us the day that we are born.

ANDROMACHE Oh Hector, but if you stay home—

HECTOR I have to go. Give me a kiss. Now go home, love. Don't cry. Pray.

POET Hector puts on his heavy helmet and goes back to the front lines. (*Tired from the knowledge of what's to come.*) Huhhh.

Have you ever seen a front line? (*Shakes his head.*) Let's take—I want to show you what that bloody field looked like, what Hector walked back to just then, with all those other boys scattered across it. It's like, it's like—I have a picture here. (*He rifles through his suitcase.*) It's from another war but—oh, I can't—(*Can't find it.*)—well here. (*He holds up his hand instead, using it as a map.*)—you see, outside the trenches where there had been a particularly bad day—this was, oh, a hundred years ago but you get the picture—and uhhh the battlefield was just littered with bodies and when you look at it you think, "Oh, well these are a bunch of bodies," but they're not just bodies 'cuz this is—this is Jamie and this is Matthew and this is Brennan and this is Paul. This is Scottie, he was nineteen, (*About Paul.*) he was twenty-one, (*About Brennan.*) he was eighteen, Brennan was meant to go to Oxford—he had gotten a scholarship because of his writing—his father was a postman. He would have been the first child in his whole family ever to go to university—but he didn't . . .

Do you see?

But this is the battle I want to tell you about now: because the women of Troy prayed, and those prayers seemed to work, and the Trojans begin to fight like never before—and still no Achilles, and that begins to take its toll on the Greeks.

This is what the war looks like:

(*The Muse provides sound that takes us there.*)

At last the armies clashed at one strategic point,
they slammed their shields together, pike scraped pike
with the grappling strength of fighters armed in bronze
and their round shields pounded, boss on welded boss,
and the sound of struggle roared and rocked the earth.
Screams of men and cries of triumph breaking in one breath,
fighters killing, fighters killed, and the ground streamed blood.
Wildly as two winter torrents raging down from the mountains,
swirling into a valley, hurl their great waters together,
plunging down in a gorge
and miles away in the hills a shepherd hears the thunder—
so from the grinding armies broke the cries and crash of war.
. . . and Terror and Rout and relentless Strife stormed too,
sister of manslaughtering Ares, Ares' comrade-in-arms—
Strife, only a slight thing when she first rears her head
but her head soon hits the sky as she strides across the earth.
Now Strife hurled down the leveler Hate amidst both sides,
wading into the onslaught, flooding men with pain.

The Trojans are weakening but after Hector takes a visit to tell people to pray for them they start to succeed, Hector also visits his wife.

50

PART FOUR

PATROCLUS

Denis O'Hare, NYTW, 2012.

POET (*Pouring a drink.*) I never could come up with the right uh . . . epithet for Patroclus.

Son of Menoetius.

Horseman.

You know what I should call him, I suppose:

Friend.

Patroclus was Achilles' friend. His only friend. They were boyhood friends. Patroclus was sent by his own father to live with Achilles' family—he's slightly older than Achilles, good with horses, and practical. His father said to Patroclus: "It's your duty to take care of Achilles. You're wiser than he is. Counsel him and he'll listen to you." And so Patroclus and Achilles were more than friends, they were brothers. And really they were more than brothers, they loved each other. When Achilles couldn't sleep, Patroclus would hold him—that kind of thing. Friends. (*A sip of whiskey.*)

Now Patroclus was a good fighter, but when Achilles retreats to his

death

tent, Patroclus stops fighting too. There's no question, his first allegiance is to his friend. But on this day, this day when Trojans are slaughtering Greeks left and right, and the Trojans have gotten past the Greek ramparts, they've crashed through all the Greek defenses, and Patroclus has been running up and down the beach, watching the bodies carried—but there's nowhere to carry them—and he sees that Agamemnon is wounded, and Odysseus is wounded, and the one medic is wounded, and he can't take it anymore. He runs to Achilles' tent:

PATROCLUS (*Catching his breath.*) Don't be mad at me—but your anger is making you blind! Can't you see that Hector is destroying us? Is your heart made of iron?

If you won't fight, drive the Trojans back, then let me. Give me your armor—they might think I'm you. I'll take that chance—but you are wrong, you will be remembered as a fool, if you won't fight this day.

ACHILLES But I swore. I won't fight for Agamemnon, I won't fight even if the Trojans sweep into my own tent. It's not even my anger now, it's the thought of breaking my word. *I can't do it.*

But you—that's a good idea. You fight in my place.

>The whole city of Troy comes trampling down on us,
>daring, wild—why? They cannot see the brow of my helmet
>flash before their eyes—

If you put on my armor . . . (*Smiling now.*) they'll think I'm back . . . just the thought I'm back in the battle will send them running in terror. Here, take it, my breastplate, my greaves, my helmet—but promise me this—you must only fight until you drive the Trojans back from our ramparts. And no further. Do not push close to the Trojan walls—not without me.

PATROCLUS   I promise.

POET   Can you see it, can you?

The young Patroclus—I can't help it, I always see him as young—too small for Achilles' armor, so that, you know, he's kind of knocking around inside it . . .

> Patroclus O my rider,
> straight at the pressing Trojan ranks you swooped . . .

(*He drains the glass.*)

And at first he does as he's promised—the sight of Achilles' armor terrifies the Trojan fighters, they lose their nerve, and Patroclus drives them back from the Argive ships, and then further, and further. He's good at this, Patroclus, he never knew he was so good at it—he's gifted, he breathes in the smell of blood and bronze, he's been waiting NINE YEARS to show what he's made of, and here he is wearing Achilles' armor and he feels GOOD, ya know?

(*Suddenly shifting his tone.*) You know that feeling when, for whatever reason, you could kill somebody? Right then and there. You could kill them. You could tear their fucking head off. You could rend them limb from limb. The guy in front of you who cuts you off, you could ram him with your car, you don't care about the result—just ram him! And you can see the charred metal and you can see the see the smoking thing and you can see the air bag and you hope the air bag smothers him. And if it doesn't, you'll get out and you'll go, "You fucking idiot! Why did you fucking cut me off?!" AAAARRRRRGGGGGHHHHHH! (*Vaulting into the battle.*)

> glint of a spear
> tore his opponent's chest
> stabbed his right jawbone, ramming the spearhead
> square between his teeth so hard—
> hoisted, dragged the Trojan—
> fury bursting his heart—
> mouth gaping—
> —flipped him down facefirst,
> dead as he fell—

(THE POET *getting into the bloodlust now.*)

Ha! Ha!

> lunging in—
> he flung a rock
> struck between his eyes
> crushed both brows,
> the skull caved in
> and both eyes burst from their sockets

(THE POET *climbs up on the table now, feverish, swaying, shouting, out of control—*)

NOTHING can hurt Patroclus now, he's a killing MACHINE, my
god—

Patroclus like something superhuman—
Patroclus and his men—
Hungry as wolves that rend and bolt raw flesh,
hearts filled with battle-frenzy that never dies—
they gorge on the kill till all their jaws drip red with blood,
belching bloody meat, but the fury, never shaken,
builds inside their chests though their glutted bellies burst—

It's a BLUR OF KILLS!! One man—SLASHED! Another—GORED!
Another—HAMMERED! Another—SPLINTERED!—SINEWS SHRED-
DED!—BRONZE RIPPING!—SPLIT THE BELLY!—RAZOR SLICING!
—Another—CUTTING AWAY THE TONGUE! One guy—CRACKED
THROUGH THE BONY SOCKET! Then—WRENCHED THE WHOLE
ARM OUT!!

(THE POET, *panting now, has the Rage Fever himself, he can't stop,
he's wild-eyed and thrashing, he's forgotten himself, caught up in
the blood lust—*)

IMPALED!! (*Urging himself on.*) More . . .
WHIPPED!! (*Urging himself on.*) More . . .
STABBED!! (*Urging himself on.*) More . . .
CHOPPED!!
SNAPPED!!
HEWED!!
SMASHED!!
HACKED!!
WHOLE EARTH RAN HOT WITH BLOOD BLOOD BLOOD.

And RED DEATH!! AND IT FEELS GOOOODD!!!!

(*He suddenly stops himself, panting. He looks out at us, desperate, lost.*)

Oh god. (*Catching his breath.*) I'm sorry . . .

I'm sorry, that's not—

Sometimes it just—

This is why I don't do this. This is why I don't do this.

(*After a long moment, he tries to find his way back to his story:*)

So Patroclus crowded corpse on corpse on the earth that rears us all.

And then . . . in the middle of it all—impossibly, like I have never quite understood what happened . . . his helmet falls off, some of his armor falls off, he suddenly gets shoved to the ground like some massive force hit him, something hit him.

His helmet didn't fit anyway. The armor didn't fit anyway. I mean, like to even put it on he had to stuff rags in his head and rags in his chest to keep the thing on. It's not his armor, it's Achilles' armor. Achilles has like four hundred pounds on him, or whatever it is.

So Patroclus, you know after all the struggling, has lost his helmet, he's lost some of his armor. I mean at the time, you know what some people said was that—Apollo knocked it off him. Apollo was on Hector's side. And that Apollo, went like this:

(*Click with wink.*)

Came up behind him and just went,

(*Click with wink.*)

With his little finger and his helmet, "Chhh."

(*Knocking off the helmet.*)

And Apollo kind of went, (*Exhale.*)

And the straps broke on the breastplate. And it fell off.

And so Patroclus stands up and goes, (*Inhale.*)

Totally exposed. And out of nowhere comes this Dardan, this guy . . . a nobody—never fought before—first day of fighting, done very very well, ya know, running around, I think he has killed nine people so far, he's knocked five chariot riders off their—uh—things. Takes his spear and literally, happens to be behind Patroclus and just kind of goes, "Uhhh." (*Makes spear-thrusting gesture.*)

Right through him. And Patroclus, like he doesn't even feel it, just kind of goes (*Turning back.*) . . . and sees this kid, this Dardan. The Dardan takes his spear (*Pulling spear out.*) pulls it back out, and runs away.

then, Patroclus, the end of life came blazing up before you—

Hector.

death

Hector sees Achilles' armor and Hector makes his move. He comes running at him, from, I don't know how far away, but he gets up a head of steam. Comes running at him, running at him, running at him. He takes his spear and, how did it work? What we say is that it went up his bowels—

—and the brazen point
went jutting straight out through Patroclus' back.

Patroclus crashes to the ground. And then Hector begins to RAGE:

HECTOR
                    Patroclus—
surely you must have thought you'd storm my city down,
you'd wrest from the wives of Troy their day of freedom,
you fool! The vultures will eat your body raw!
Not for all his power could Achilles save you now—
and how he must have filled your ears with orders
—you maniac, you obeyed!!

POET   And then Patroclus—holding his body together with his hands—Patroclus curses Hector.

PATROCLUS.
. . . you won't live long yourself, I swear.
Already I see them looming up beside you—death
and the strong force of fate, to bring you down—

POET   (*A simple funeral ritual.*)
Death cut him short. The end closed in around him.
Flying free of his limbs
his soul went winging down to the House of Death.

But Hector can't stop yelling at Patroclus, even though he's dead:

HECTOR   You think you know my *fate*?? Why should I fear Death? No. Death is on *my* side. He is *my brother*. And together we will devastate you, we will murder all Greeks!

POET
> With that he planted a heel against Patroclus' chest,
> wrenched his brazen spear from the wound, kicked him over,
> flat on his back —

And then he tears the rest of Achilles' armor off the dead body, savagely, awkwardly, crying out like an animal.

Hector is . . . a good guy, an honorable man. But at that moment— well . . .

(*With some shame about his own infection.*) Yes. That's how it happens. We think of ourselves: not me, I'm not like that, I'm a peaceful—

but it happens anyway, some trick in our blood and—

(*A fierce whisper.*) —rage.

Do you see?

(*He pours the rest of the bottle into the glass, gulps it down.*)

Achillies refuces to fight Causing his beft frend to go out for him and die.

PART FIVE

ACHILLES' NEW SHIELD

Denis O'Hare, NYTW, 2012.

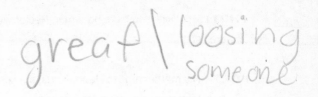

great \ loosing someone

POET

A black cloud of grief came shrouding over Achilles.
Overpowered in all his power, sprawled in the dust,
Achilles suddenly loosed a terrible, wrenching cry
And his noble mother heard him . . .

Here is what Achilles says to his mother:

ACHILLES He's dead. And I sent him out there. It should have
been me. What do I do now?

If only strife could die from the lives of gods and men
and anger that drives the sanest man to flare in outrage—
bitter gall, sweeter than dripping streams of honey,
that swarms in people's chests and blinds like smoke—
just like the anger Agamemnon king of men
has roused within me now . . .

                                    Enough.
Let bygones be bygones. Done is done.

Now I'll go and meet that murderer head-on,
that Hector who destroyed the dearest life I know.

65

THETIS   Wait—you have no armor, Hector wears your armor now. Sit here, wait.

POET   His mother runs to Hephaestus, the crippled god of fire, and asks him to make new armor for Achilles.

Hephaestus flicks his hand and tripods swing into place. He waves his hand again and twenty bellows begin pumping and blowing on the fires and the coals start to glow white hot. Again and again he waves his hands and tin, bronze, gold, silver fly through the air, plunging into cauldrons, to be melted down for Achilles—a breastplate, greaves for his legs, a helmet made of bronze and a shield—the most magnificent shield I've ever seen. Hephaestus begins to fashion an immense orb—a shield as big as a room—with the river of the Ocean circling . . . he puts the earth, the sky, the oceans, the sun, the moon, all the stars. He hammers out two cities on this shield: in one there is a wedding taking place, a bride is led down a hillock past trees to her nervous groom—a city at peace. The other city is a walled city and outside it a siege is going on—two armies clash by a river. He fashions a field, large with furrows and he shows the horses tilling back and forth and the farmers being refreshed with large cups of wine and honey—a farmer bringing home his cattle and a lion attacks one of the bulls, and black blood pools on the bottom of the shield—a boy playing a lyre—heartbreaking music—a song of the dying day—a circle of boys and girls dancing, with a crowd gathered around, clapping, singing, laughing.

This is Achilles' new shield and it gleamed with a, with a beam that it— it—it went so far. It was as if you were—you were, you were far out at sea, you know, a sailor when they have to look out at the shore and try to find their bearings and they look for a light and you have lighthouses now—but then, sometimes, we would have, like a—one guy on a mountain, herding his sheep and he would have a very strong light, you know, to try to . . . keep the sailors, sailors safe. And . . . and they're way out at sea, and this light beam comes flying out. That's how Achilles' shield looked from a distance. It—it—it just bounced the light back, shot it way out like that.

(*A great wind kicks up, and quickly grows.*)

When Achillies plans on taking revenge, Hephaetus, the God of fire, makes him new amazing armer, and the biggest, best shield ever made.

PART SIX

HECTOR'S DEATH

Brian Ellingsen, Perth Festival, Australia, 2014.

POET

> Achilles . . . dashed toward the city,
> heart racing . . . rushing on
> like a champion stallion drawing a chariot full tilt,
> sweeping across the plain in easy, tearing strides—
> so Achilles hurtled on, driving legs and knees.
>
> And Hector was first to see him coming,
> surging over the plain, blazing like a star.

And I don't have to tell you, do I?—The tide has turned, of course, because Achilles is back in the game. The Greeks are winning, raging, driving the Trojans back inside their own walls.

> But there stood Hector,
> shackled fast by his deadly fate, holding his ground,
> exposed in front of Troy and the Scaean Gates.

71

This is what he looks like. (*Holding his ground.*) And this is what he's
thinking:

HECTOR

> No way out. If I slip inside the gates and walls . . .
> Now my army's ruined . . .
> I would die of shame to face the men of Troy
> and the Trojan women trailing
> their long robes . . .
>   So now, better by far for me
> to stand up to Achilles, kill him, come home alive
> or die at his hands in glory out before the walls.

POET   And then he stops—listen:

HECTOR

> But wait—what if I put down my studded shield
> and heavy helmet, prop my spear on the rampart
> and go forth, just as I am, to meet Achilles . . .
> why, I could promise to give back Helen, yes,
> and all her treasures with her, all those riches
> Paris once hauled home to Troy in the hollow ships—
> and they were the cause of all our endless fighting—

POET   And that's what we've all been thinking, isn't it? Isn't it?
JUST GIVE HER BACK!!!

HECTOR

> Yes, yes, return it all to the sons of Atreus now
> to haul away, and then, at the same time, divide
> the rest with all the Argives, all the city holds,

and then I'd take an oath for the Trojan royal council
that we will hide nothing! Share and share alike the hoards
our handsome citadel stores within its depths and—

(*He stops.*) Why debate, my friend? Why thrash things out?
No way to parley with that man—not now—
not from behind some oak or rock to whisper,
like a boy and a young girl, lovers' secrets
a boy and girl might whisper to each other . . .
Better to clash in battle, now, at once—

POET

                                    So he wavered,
waiting there, but Achilles was closing on him now
like the god of war, the fighter's helmet flashing,
over his right shoulder shaking the Pelian ash spear,
that terror, and the bronze around his body flared
like a raging fire or the rising, blazing sun.
Hector looked up, saw him, started to tremble,
nerve gone, he could hold his ground no longer,
he left the gates behind and away he fled in fear—
so Achilles flew at him, breakneck on in fury
with Hector fleeing along the walls of Troy,
fast as his legs would go. On and on they raced,
passing the lookout point, passing the wild fig tree
tossed by the wind, always out from under the ramparts
down the wagon trail they careered until they reached
the clear running springs where whirling Scamander
rises up from its double wellsprings bubbling strong—
Past these they raced, one escaping, one in pursuit
and the one who fled was great but the one pursuing

greater, even greater—their pace mounting in speed
like powerful stallions—so the two of them
whirled three times around the city of Priam,
sprinting at top speed.

                And Hector could never throw
Achilles off his trail, the swift racer Achilles—
time and again he'd make a dash for the Dardan Gates,
trying to rush beneath the rock-built ramparts, hoping
men on the heights might save him, somehow, raining spears
but time and again Achilles would intercept him quickly,
heading him off, forcing him out across the plain
and always sprinting along the city side himself—
endless as in a dream . . .
when a man can't catch another fleeing on ahead
and he can never escape nor his rival overtake him—
so the one could never run the other down in his speed
nor the other spring away. And how could Hector have fled
the fates of death so long?

(THE POET *holds out his hands.)* This is the scale the gods use to weigh the fates of men. Zeus weighs the fates of Hector and Achilles in the scales—and these are real, actual things, these scales—and down went Hector's day of doom, dragging him down to the strong House of Death—and the gods left him.

HECTOR (*Exhausted, panting:*)
No more running from you in fear, Achilles!
Now my spirit stirs me
to meet you face-to-face. Now kill or be killed!
Come, we'll swear to the gods, the highest witnesses—
if Zeus allows me to last it out and tear your life away,

Power

I will give your body back to your loyal comrades.
Swear you'll do the same.

ACHILLES

Hector, stop!
There are no binding oaths between men and lions—
wolves and lambs can enjoy no meeting of the minds—
they are all bent on hating each other to the death.
So with you and me—

POET (*Stepping aside from the action.*) Oh! If you could see the way
they look at each other . . .

What do they see?

(*An intense whisper.*) I wonder if he's scared—look at him, he may
be yelling and shaking his spear but when it comes right down to it
he wants to stay alive. And I can even imagine, we could leave here,
now, we'll get drunk together somewhere and we'll talk about like, "Hey
remember that battle, when was it four days ago when you guys had
us pinned against the wall and then out of nowhere that young spear-
man got your charioteer and you guys got thrown . . . that was intense."
"Yeah, yeah, and how 'bout that bird that came out of nowhere, that
was kinda freaky." "Yeah, that thing just landed in the middle of the
field and for a minute we were all staring at it. Was it a heron?" "No no
no, it was an egret." "Oh we call 'em herons." "No, isn't the heron with
the blue tinge to its upper wings?" "Weeellll, uhhh, I think we call *that*
an egret . . . "

But . . . no. Whatever he may have been thinking, this is what Achilles
said:

Anger

ACHILLES

>   Now you'll pay at a stroke for all my comrades' grief,
>   all you killed in the fury of your spear!

POET

>   With that,
>   shaft poised, Achilles hurled and his spear's long shadow flew
>   but seeing it coming glorious Hector ducked away,
>   crouching down, watching the bronze tip fly past
>   and stab the earth . . .

HECTOR

>   You missed, look—the great godlike Achilles!
>   All bluff, cunning with words, that's all you are—
>   But now it's for you to dodge my brazen spear—

POET

>   Shaft poised, he hurled and his spear's long shadow flew
>   and it struck Achilles' shield—a dead-center hit—
>   but off and away it glanced and Hector seethed,
>   his hurtling spear, his whole arm's power poured
>   in a wasted shot. He stood there, cast down . . .
>   he had no spear in reserve . . .
>   . . . Yes and Hector knew the truth in his heart
>   and the fighter cried aloud,

HECTOR

>   My time has come!
>   And now death, grim death is looming up beside me,
>   no longer far away. No way to escape it now.

> Well let me die—
> but not without struggle, not without glory, no,
> in some great clash of arms that even men to come
> will hear of down the years!

POET

> And on that resolve
> Hector swooped now, swinging his whetted sword
> and Achilles charged too, bursting with rage, barbaric.
> And fire flared from the sharp point of the spear Achilles
> brandished high in his right hand, bent on Hector's death,
> scanning his splendid body—where to pierce it best?
> The rest of his flesh seemed all encased in armor,
> burnished, brazen—Achilles' armor that Hector stripped
> from strong Patroclus when he killed him—

That's right! Hector is wearing Achilles' armor, my god, and so there is Achilles, spear in hand, and he's looking at himself, in a way, at an image of himself—he's looking for a weak spot, and he knows exactly where that is, *'cause it's his armor* . . .

> . . . one spot lay exposed,
> where collarbones lift the neckbone off the shoulders,
> the open throat, where the end of life comes quickest—*there*
> as Hector charged in fury, brilliant Achilles drove his spear
> and the point went stabbing clean through the tender neck . . .
> Hector crashed in the dust—
> godlike Achilles gloried over him:

ACHILLES

Hector—surely you thought when you stripped Patroclus' armor

that you, you would be safe! Never a fear of me—
far from the fighting as I was—you fool!
The dogs and birds will maul you, shame your corpse
while Achaeans bury my dear friend in glory!

POET

Struggling for breath, Hector, his helmet flashing, said,

HECTOR

I beg you, beg you by your life, your parents—
don't let the dogs devour me by the Argive ships!
Wait, take the princely ransom of bronze and gold,
the gifts my father and noble mother will give you—
but give my body to friends to carry home again—

ACHILLES

Beg no more, you fawning dog—begging me by my parents!
Would to god my rage, my fury would drive me now
to hack your flesh away and eat you raw—
such agonies you have caused me! Ransom?

The dogs and birds will rend you—blood and bone!

HECTOR

I know you well—I see my fate before me.
Iron inside your chest, that heart of yours.
But now beware, or my curse will draw god's wrath
upon your head, that day when Paris and lord Apollo—
for all your fighting heart—destroy you at the Scaean Gates!

POET   (*Performing a brief ritual.*)

Death cut him short. The end closed in around him.
Flying free of his limbs
his soul went winging down to the House of Death.

ACHILLES   (*Doing a kind of victory dance.*)

Now,
come, you sons of Achaea, raise a song of triumph!
Down to the ships we march and bear this corpse on high—
we have won ourselves great glory. We have brought
magnificent Hector down, that man the Trojans
glorified in their city like a god!

POET

So he triumphed
and now he was bent on outrage, on shaming noble Hector.
Piercing the tendons, ankle to heel behind both feet,
he knotted straps of rawhide through them both,
lashed them to his chariot, left the head to drag
and mounting the car,
he whipped his team to a run and breakneck on they flew,
holding nothing back. And a thick cloud of dust rose up
from the man they dragged, his dark hair swirling round
that head so handsome once, all tumbled low in the dust . . .

So his whole head was dragged down in the dust.

It's so—(*He shakes his head.*)—if you'd seen it, the—the waste . . . Just
like . . . (*He blinks, seems to have lost his place.*) there was one time
. . . uhhhh . . . (*Trying to remember.*) . . . yes yes (*Shakes himself.*) . . . it

was a terrible hot day during the Conquest of Sumer—(*He stops to correct himself.*)—I mean the Conquest of Sargon—uh—the Persian War—no—

the Peloponnesian War
War of Alexander the Great
Punic War
Gallic War
Caesar's invasion of Britain
Great Jewish Revolt
Yellow Turban Rebellion
War against the Moors in North Africa
Roman-Persian War
Fall of Rome
Byzantine-Arab War
Muslim Conquest of Egypt
First Siege of Constantinople
Arab-Chinese War
Saxon Wars
Viking raids across Europe
Bulgarian Siege of Constantinople
Zanj Rebellion in southern Iraq
Croatian-Bulgarian War
Viking Civil War
Norman Conquest of England
First Crusade
Second Crusade
Third Crusade
Fourth Crusade
Children's Crusade

Fifth
Sixth
Seventh
Eighth
Ninth Crusade
Norman invasion of Ireland
Mongol invasion of China
Mongol invasion of Russia
Mongol invasion of Afghanistan
Mongol invasion of Vietnam
The Hundred Years' War
Chinese Domination of Vietnam
Polish-Lithuanian-Teutonic War
Hunger War
Fall of Constantinople
Wars of the Roses
War of the Priests
Muscovite-Lithuanian Wars
The Spanish Conquest of Mexico
The Mughal Conquest of India
War of the Two Brothers
The Spanish Conquest of Peru
Thirty Years' War
Pequot War
First, Second and Third English Civil Wars
Cromwell's conquest of Ireland
Cromwell's conquest of Scotland
The 335 Years' War
French and Indian Wars
Second Cherokee War
American Revolution

French Revolution

Haitian Revolution

The Napoleonic Wars

The Bolivian War of Independence

Argentine War of Independence

Mexican War of Independence

Venezuelan War of Independence

War of 1812

Colombian, Chilean, Peruvian, and Ecuadorian Wars of Independence

Lower Canada Rebellion

Upper Canada Rebellion

Second Seminole War

Mormon War

Pastry War

Honey War

First Anglo-Afghan War

First Opium War

The Land Wars

Crimean War

American Civil War

Sioux Wars

Second Anglo-Afghan War

The Boer Wars

Cuban War of Independence

Spanish-American War

Mexican Revolution

World War I

Russian Revolution

Third Anglo-Afghan War

Irish War of Independence

Afghan Civil War

Japanese Invasion of Manchuria
Saudi-Yemeni War
Spanish Civil War
World War II
Palestine Civil War
Arab-Israeli War
Cold War
Korean War
Cuban Revolution
Tibetan Rebellion
Vietnam
Bay of Pigs
Sand War
Six-Day War
Laos
Cambodia
The Troubles
Prague Spring
Nicaraguan Revolution
Salvadoran Civil War
Soviet Invasion of Afghanistan
Contra war in Nicaragua
Second Sudanese Civil War
Iran-Iraq War
Falklands War
Israeli Invasion of Lebanon
U.S. Invasion of Grenada
U.S. Invasion of Panama
First Intifada
Afghan Civil War
Rwandan Civil War

Bosnia and Herzegovina
Chechnya
Afghanistan
Kosovo
Iraq
Chechnya
Afghanistan
Rwanda
Darfur
Iraq
Haiti
Pakistan
Lebanon
Kenya
Zimbabwe
Congo
Gaza
Somalia
Georgia
Iraq
Pakistan
Afghanistan
Libya
Syria . . . *

Achillies kills Hector in order to avenge his friend Patroclus.

* As time goes on, it may be necessary to add a war or wars at the end of the list to reflect current events. This should be done with great restraint and include only major conflicts. The same is true of the list of destroyed cities toward the end of the play.

FUNERAL GAMES

Denis O'Hare, NYTW, 2012.

THE POET *is slumped in the chair, lost. He lifts his head, sees the audience and makes his way back to the story.*

POET | Hecuba | opens her mouth:

Because all this time, uhhh . . . they were all watching—the Trojans, from the top of the rampart: his mother Hecuba, his father, his brothers, Helen. All of the Trojans, watching Hector die.

(THE POET *opens his mouth and lets out a cry.*) Oooooooooohhh . . .

(THE POET *begins to wail in Ancient Greek—great, sung sorrow.*)

τέκνον ἐγὼ δειλή: τί νυ βείομαι αἰνὰ παθοῦσα
TEK non eh | GO DEI | LEH ti nu | BEI o mai | AI na pa | THOU sa
σεῦ   ποτεθνηῶτος;
SEU ah po | TETH NEH | O tos? . . .
νῦν αὖ θάνατος καὶ μοῖρα κιχάνει.
. . . NUN | AU tha na | TOS // KAI | MOI ra ki | KHA NEI

[*Translation:*
  My child—my desolation! How can I go on living?
  . . . now death and fate have seized you dragged you down!]

87

And all around the ramparts, Hector's family wailed with the grieving Hecuba.

But his wife, Andromache, wasn't at the wall, she was inside weaving, she hadn't seen a thing. Busy drawing his bath . . . she'd talked herself into the idea that he was coming home, he'd need a bath . . .

. . . then she hears the women wailing, she hears her mother-in-law's voice, she recognizes that voice—she's never, ever, heard that voice sound like that before—her heart pounds, her legs go numb—

ANDROMACHE
　　　　　　　—Oh I know it . . .
something terrible's coming down on Priam's children.

POET　That's an awful moment, isn't it? It starts with uhh, a bad feeling or an intuition or why did the phone ring at 3 o'clock in the morning? Or I didn't get a phone call, or, he didn't come home or it's late, it's really late, he should have been home by now, I should have heard by now, the plane should have landed by now, he should have called . . .

She starts to walk, trying to keep herself calm, trying not to panic—but her heart begins to race and she starts getting that weird throbbing and she starts, her eyes start to go kinda dim—she can't actually see where she's going—and she comes out and even before she gets to ask a question she looks out across the plain and she actually sees her husband, dead, being dragged behind the chariot—

And she starts to yell at him—

ANDROMACHE

Now you go down
to the House of Death, the dark depths of the earth,
and leave me here to waste away in grief, a widow
lost in the royal halls—and the boy only a baby.

Hector, what help are you to him, now you are dead?
What help is he to you? Think, even if he escapes
the wrenching horrors of war against the Argives,
pain and labor will plague him all his days to come.

POET You know what she's really saying? She's saying:

I told you so.

Hector's body disappears in a cloud of dust.

Achilles drags his prize to the Greek camp and dumps it in the sand—next to the Argive ships. The Greeks cheer and drink and celebrate. But Achilles' fury just won't end . . . and so he drags Hector's body round and round Patroclus' tomb, day after day after day. And the thing you have to ask yourself is: It's been TEN DAYS!!!!! What's there left to drag?

(THE POET *shakes his head.*) No no no, you'd be wrong, see, because THE GODS. The gods look down and—I mean really, after all their meddling, after leaving Hector to die, well now they change their minds . . .

They wrap Hector's body in—oh, a magic shield of STORM—Zeus loves him after all—and so Hector's body is perfect, just—unharmed. Sweet-smelling.

Impossible.

So. For ten days, the Trojans have been watching from a distance: the dust rising, funeral pyres smoking, the Greeks carousing and singing songs of the Triumph of Achilles. And . . . and Hector's father, Priam, decides to go—even though he's almost *eighty years old*—he decides to slog through all the battlefields to the Greek camp, to ransom himself, his kingdom, all his treasures, to Achilles to get his son's body back.

He sets off with only one old charioteer in the middle of the night. It's dark and dangerous and—just as Priam and his driver start getting tired, a young man with *fabulous sandals* appears in front of them.

HERMES   What are you old guys up to—? You're crossing into Greek territory now, you're about to cross enemy lines—with your wagon full of treasure. You've lost your minds. Listen (*Wink.*)—I'll help you, I'll show you the way.

POET   Priam asks him who he is. But the young man goes . . . (*Shhh . . . finger to lips.*).

They sweep unseen across the battlefield, past the ramparts, past the sentries and when they get to the massive gate—so big that it usually takes eight men to push open the doors—the young man, their guide, simply whistles (*He whistles.*) and the gates fly open.

HERMES   Old man, I'll tell you who I am. I am Hermes. (Wink.) And I can go no further.

POET   Then he's gone. (*Snap.*) Priam looks up to see Achilles—

standing up from the dinner table. It's like staring into the face of a deathless god. Breathtaking.

PRIAM Great Achilles—You are surprised to see me here, an old man. I am Priam, King of Troy.

I've driven a wagon, full of treasure, all the way here from my city. I will ransom—everything . . . Look how I kneel at your feet.

> I have endured what no one on earth has ever done before —
> I put to my lips the hand of the man who killed my son.

POET Achilles says, he says—

ACHILLES You amaze me, old man. Get up!! Don't kneel at my feet!

PRIAM You have a father. Remember *your* father. You're so far away from home, your father's probably suffering right now, no one is there to help him. Your father needs you, and you're far away in Troy. What would *he* give to have you home with him? I'm asking you now, as your father would ask me, give me the body. Let me have the body of my son.

ACHILLES I never cried before I came to Troy. But in these last forty days, I find myself crying almost every day. I have reason to cry— and so do you, old man.

POET And they both start to weep . . . Priam crying for his dead son, Achilles crying for his aging father, so far away, and for his dead friend, Patroclus, and for himself.

ACHILLES Enough. Enough grief, enough tears. What good will our tears do? I won't see my father again. You can't bring your son back to life.

PRIAM (*Springing up.*) Give me my son! You took him from me! His body is rotting out there on the beach—I've had enough of this—LET ME SEE MY SON!

ACHILLES (*A dark glance.*) Don't make me mad. You don't know—the way my heart is—so full of rage—I'm sick with it, old man—don't stir my rage, don't make me angry, or I'll—

POET And now here's the thing. What I love singing, and I hope I can make you see: For once, Achilles, who is addicted to rage—as so many of us are, really, when it comes right down to it—this fighting man feels the rage well up in his heart . . . and he makes it disappear.

He just—(THE POET *breathes out, showing how Achilles lets go of his rage.*)

How did he do that?

Achilles lets go of his rage, and goes outside, and he lifts Hector up in his own arms . . .

(THE POET *raises his arms as if carrying the broken body.*)

. . . Achilles lifted Hector up in his own arms—

And laid him down in his father's wagon.

ACHILLES   OK, it's done. I've laid him in your wagon, old man.
No—don't run out there now—I'll have my men make a bed for you,
out on the porch—in the morning, you will see him, and then you'll
take him home. Oh—one more thing: How many days do you need to
bury Prince Hector?

PRIAM   (*Taken aback.*) Well, we need time to set up his memorial
. . . our city is far from the hills—we'd have to go out and haul in timber
for the pyre . . . we'd need nine days to mourn him, and then we'd bury
him on the tenth day, and one more day to finish his tomb, and have a
feast in his honor . . . eleven days. We would need eleven days. And then
we could fight again on the twelfth day . . . if that's absolutely necessary.

ACHILLES   Done. You'll have your 11 days. I'll make the Greeks
stop fighting for 11 days.

PRIAM   (*Beat.*) Put me to bed.

POET   Priam reached out his hand, and Achilles took it, and led the
old man to the porch. Priam slept, dreaming of the journey home, and
Achilles slept, dreaming of his father, and the entire Greek army slept,
dreaming of the next day's battle . . .

. . . and the sentries guarding the walls of Troy slept, and all of the
Trojan civilians slept, and all of the Trojan soldiers slept. And in the
countryside, the farmers and the shepherds and the animals slept,
and in the Greek ships the slaves and the oarsmen slept, and even,
way up on Olympus, Zeus lay his head on Hera's shoulder, and even
the gods fell asleep . . .

(*Pause.*)

I don't want to tell you about what happens next—I know you know—about the trick that did it—the Trojan Horse—I can't do it—(*He starts packing up.*) how the Greeks pretended to leave, and Troy rejoiced and they thought it was over, the war was over—but that night Greek soldiers snuck out—and began the slaughter and the burning—the Sack of Troy, that's not—I'm not singing that song . . . the song of the murder of Priam, the song of the death of Achilles . . . the song of Hector's infant son thrown from the battlements—how the Greek soldier held him up in one hand, but the baby laughed, the soldier's helmet made him think of his father, and this time he thought it was a game—the sound of the boy's head splitting on the pavement . . . (*He turns to get his coat.*) the song of the Trojan women, all of them kidnapped and raped and taken to Greece, the song of Aeneas escaping with his father on his back, the song of Odysseus, trying to get home, no, it's too much, all these songs . . .

(*Grabbing his suitcase.*) Imagine it for yourselves, the destruction of a city, a civilization, you know what that looks like . . . like . . .

. . . Alexandria, all that history lost . . . (*Pause, searching . . .*)

. . . like . . .

. . . Constantinople, burning for weeks . . .

. . . like . . .

. . . the Aztec temples, razed . . .

. . . like . . .

Dresden . . . Hiroshima . . .

like . . .

Sarajevo . . .

like . . .

Kabul . . .

like . . .

(THE POET *stops. He seems to crumple, becoming a sad ancient pile of dust. After some moments, he stumbles up. He shuffles over to an old sink—and turns on the water. He splashes water on his face then takes a deep breath. He comes back downstage.*)

I will tell you this:

Cassandra saw them first. Priam and the wagon and the body of Hector.

Priam told his people of the cease-fire, not to worry, there would be no war for eleven whole days, they could bury Hector the proper way. And so they built a pyre, and they mourned him, and on the tenth night they burned his body—until the sun came up.

(*Taking another step closer to the audience.*)   At last,
when young Dawn with her rose-red fingers shone once more,
the people massed around illustrious Hector's pyre . . .
And once they'd gathered, crowding the meeting grounds,
they first put out the fires with glistening wine,
wherever the flames still burned in all their fury.
Then they collected the white bones of Hector—
all his brothers, his friends-in-arms, mourning,
and warm tears came streaming down their cheeks.
They placed the bones they found in a golden chest,
shrouding them round and round in soft purple cloths.

Death

They quickly lowered the chest in a deep, hollow grave
and over it piled a cope of huge stones closely set,
then hastily heaped a barrow, posted lookouts all around
for fear the Achaen combat troops would launch their attack
before the time agreed.

(*Slowly, with ceremony.*) And once they'd heaped the mound
they turned back home to Troy, and gathering once again
they shared a splendid funeral feast in Hector's honor,
held in the house of Priam, king by will of Zeus.

ς οἵ γ᾽ μφίεπον τάφον Ἕκτορος ἱπποδάμοιο
HOS HOI | G'AM phi eh | PON ta phon | HEK toros | HI ppo da | MOI o

And so the Trojans buried Hector breaker of horses.

(THE POET *stands there for a moment, silent. He looks out at the audience, expectantly.*)

You see?

(*Blackout.*)

END OF PLAY

Hector is finally buried and Hectors father and Achilles talk and finally agree.